GERMAN FOOTBALL STADIUMS

daab

Hamburg
Berlin
Hannover
Gelsenkirchen
Dortmund
Leipzig
Köln
Frankfurt
Kaiserslautern
Nürnberg
Stuttgart
München

Fußball in Deutschland - das heißt Bundesliga zwischen Bayern München und Schalke 04 oder Hertha BSC Berlin gegen den Hamburger SV. Das heißt auch Champions League und UEFA Cup sowie internationale Spiele der Nationalmannschaften. Fußball in Deutschland – das sind gesellschaftliche Orte, an denen sich lokale Identität und Sozialgeschichte kristallisieren. Moderne Stadien sind bauliche Meisterwerke fokusiert auf Forschung, Logistik, Statik, Flexibilität und Emotion. Stadion dieser Größe müssen innerhalb weniger Minuten tausende von Besuchern aufnehmen, müssen die Sicherheit der riesigen Konstruktionsflächen bei Wind und Wetter garantieren und sie müssen gleichzeitig ihrem Publikum das Gefühl der Heiterkeit, des Stolzes und der Verbundenheit mit diesem Stadion vermitteln. Und zu guter Letzt sind Fußballstadien wohl der letzte Ort, der alle gesellschaftlichen Klassen versammelt. Arbeiter, Schüler, Rentner, Politiker, Wirtschaftsbosse, Mittelständler – allesamt vereint auf den Tribünen der Stadien.

Soccer in Germany – that means Bundesliga action between Bayern Munich and Schalke 04 or Hertha BSC Berlin against Hamburger SV. It also means the Champions League and UEFA Cup, as well as the international games between the national teams. Soccer in Germany – it means social places where local identity and social history crystallize. Modern stadiums are architectural masterpieces focused on research, logistics, statics, flexibility and emotion. Stadiums of this magnitude must be capable of admitting thousands of spectators within just a few minutes, they must ensure the safety of the giant structural surfaces in all kinds of weather, and, at the same time, they must provide visitors with the feeling of optimism, pride and a connection with the stadium. Last but not least, soccer stadiums are probably the last remaining places in which all social classes meet. Laborers, students, retirees, politicians, CEOs, entrepreneurs – all are united on the stadium stands.

Le fooftball en Allemagne - ce sont des matchs de Bundesliga entre le Bayern München et Schalke 04 ou entre Hertha BSC Berlin et le Hamburger SV. C'est aussi la Ligue des Champions et la Coupe UEFA ainsi que des rencontres internationales des équipes allemandes. Le football dans ce pays - ce sont aussi des lieux de rencontre où se cristallisent l'identité locale et l'histoire sociale. Les stades modernes sont de véritables œuvres d'art de l'architecture, focalisés sur la recherche, la logistique, le calcul statique des structures, la flexibilité et l'émotion. Des stades de cette taille doivent pouvoir accueillir en quelques minutes des milliers de visiteurs, garantir la sécurité de ces immenses constructions quel que soit le temps, mais ils doivent donner aussi au public un sentiment de gaité, de fierté et de solidarité avec eux. Pour conclure enfin, les stades de football sont aujourd'hui apparemment le dernier lieu où toutes les classes sociales se retrouvent. Ouvriers, écoliers, retraités, politiciens, grands chefs d'entreprise, classes moyennes - tous réunis sur les tribunes des stades.

Fútbol en Alemania es sinónimo de Bundesliga disputada entre los equipos Bayern München y Schalke 04 o Hertha BSC Berlin y Hamburger SV. También se asocia a la Liga de Campeones y a la Copa de la UEFA, así como a los partidos internacionales disputados entre las selecciones nacionales. El fútbol en Alemania representa, a su vez, puntos de encuentro social, en los que se cristaliza la identidad local y la historia social. Los estadios modernos son obras maestras arquitectónicas que se concentran en la investigación, logística, estática, flexibilidad y emoción. Los estadios de esta envergadura tienen que ser capaces de dar cabida en pocos minutos a miles de visitantes, además, tienen que garantizar la seguridad de las enormes superficies constructivas bajo cualquier condición climática y, a su vez, proporcionar al público una sensación de alegría, orgullo y apego al respectivo estadio. Por último, los estadios de fútbol posiblemente sean el último lugar de encuentro de todas las clases sociales. Trabajadores, alumnos, jubilados, políticos, empresarios, miembros de la clase media - todos ellos reunidos en las tribunas de los estadios.

Il calcio in Germania – significa campionato nazionale tra Bayern München e Schalke 04 oppure tra Hertha BSC e Hamburger SV. Significa pure Champions League e Coppa Uefa nonché partite internazionali delle squadre nazionali. Il calcio in Germania – si svolge in luoghi pubblici dove l'identità locale e la storia sociale cristallizzano. Gli stadi moderni sono capolavori architettonici, focalizzati sulla ricerca, la logistica, la statica, la flessibilità e l'emozione. Gli stadi di queste dimensioni devono poter raccogliere migliaia di spettatori in pochi minuti, devono garantire la protezione delle enormi superfici costruttive contro il maltempo e, contemporaneamente devono regalare al pubblico la sensazione di serenità, l'orgoglio e l'attaccamento a questo stadio. E finalmente gli stadi di calcio sono probabilmente l'ultimo luogo che riunisce tutte le classi sociali. Operai, studenti, pensionati, politici, alti dirigenti dell'industria, gente appartenente al ceto medio – tutti quanti riuniti sulle tribune degli stadi.

Futebol na Alemanha é Bundesliga entre Bayern München e Schalke 04, ou Hertha BSC Berlin contra o Hamburger SV. Futebol na Alemanha também é Champions League, UEFA Cup e jogos internacionais das seleções. E futebol na Alemanha é o encontro de todas as classes sociais, a cristalização de identidades regionais, e moderna história social. Estádios de futebol modernos são obras primas baseadas em pesquisa, logística, estática, flexibilidade e emoção. Nestes modernos estádios de grandes dimensões, multidões até então inimagináveis tem de afluir em poucos minutos. Além disso, é necessário garantir a segurança de enormes áreas de construção expostas a ventos e adversidades climáticas. Mas nenhum estádio está completo se não transmitir ao público uma sensação de alegria, de orgulho e de ligação emocional com o estádio do seu time. Os estádios de futebol provavelmente são o último local onde ainda se reúnem todas as classes sociais: trabalhadores, alunos, aposentados, políticos, os poderosos do setor econômico, classe média, todos torcendo por um mesmo time.

OLYMPIASTADION
Berlin | 2004
gmp Architekten – von Gerkan, Mark und Partner | Hamburg
Schlaich Bergermann und Partner (SE) | Stuttgart
Krebs und Kiefer (SE) | Darmstadt

Olympiastadion Berlin | Olympischer Platz 3 | 14053 Berlin
www.olympiastadion-berlin.de
Mainclub: Hertha BSC Berlin
Capacity: 74.400

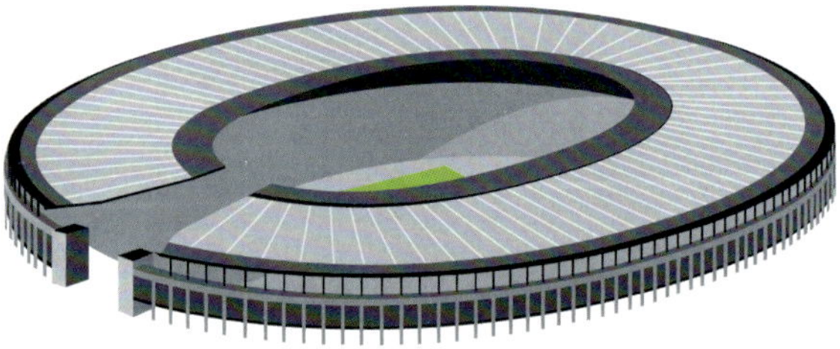

Das Olympiastadion wurde anlässlich der Olympischen Sommerspiele 1936 erbaut. Am selben Ort befand sich zuvor das Deutsche Stadion, das anlässlich der für 1916 geplanten Olympischen Spiele errichtet wurde. Nun wurde das Olympiastadion grundlegend umgebaut und modernisiert. Bei den Umbauarbeiten waren die konservatorischen Belange des Denkmalschutzes zu beachten. Umgesetzt wurde eine Gedenkstätte, die den heutigen internationalen Anforderungen an einem modernen Veranstaltungsort übertrifft und trotzdem in ruhigen Stunden einen historischen Rückblick auf Geschichte und Baukunst zulässt.

The Olympic Stadium was built for the 1936 Summer Olympic Games. It was erected on the same spot as the previous German Stadium, built for the Olympic Games planned in 1916. Now the Olympic Stadium has been renovated and modernized. During renovation work, the conservational aspects of monument protection were observed. A memorial was achieved that exceeds today‘s international requirements for modern venues and yet, in quiet moments, still allows a look back on the history and architecture.

L‘ « Olympiastadion » a été construit à l‘occasion des Jeux Olympiques d‘été de 1936, à l‘emplacement même du « Deutsches Stadion » qui, lui, avait été érigé pour les Jeux Olympiques prévus en 1916. L‘ « Olympiastadion » a maintenant été transformé et modernisé de fond en comble. Les travaux ont été effectués dans le plus grand respect du caractère historique de ce site On a ainsi construit un lieu commémoratif plus que conforme aux critères internationaux auxquels doit répondre tout site de manifestation moderne mais qui permet toutefois, une fois l‘euphorie sportive retombée, une rétrospective de l‘histoire et de l‘architecture.

El Olympiastadion (Estadio Olímpico) fue construido con motivo de los Juegos Olímpicos de Verano de 1936. En este mismo lugar se encontró en su día el Deutsche Stadion (Estadio Alemán), que a su vez fue erigido con motivo de los Juegos Olímpicos que se planeaba celebrar en 1916. El Olympiastadion se acaba de reformar y modernizar a fondo. En las obras de reconstrucción hubieron de tenerse en cuenta los requisitos de conservación establecidos por la protección del patrimonio nacional. El resultado es un lugar conmemorativo que supera los requisitos internacionales actuales que ha de satisfacer todo centro moderno de celebración de actos, y que además permite una mirada retrospectiva a la historia y la arquitectura en los momentos de tranquilidad.

L'Olympiastadion fu costruito per i giochi olimpici estivi del 1936. Nello stesso luogo prima si trovava il Deutsche Stadion che fu eretto in occasione dei giochi olimpici estivi programmati per il 1916. Ora l'Olympiastadion è stato ricostruito e modernizzato a fondo. I lavori di ricostruzione si svolsero in pieno rispetto di quanto necessario per tutelare il monumento. È stato quindi realizzato un monumento commemorativo che supera le esigenze internazionali relative ad un moderno stabilimento per grandi manifestazioni; ciononostante durante le ore tranquille permette uno sguardo retrospettivo sulla storia e l'arte architettonica.

O Olympiastadion foi construído por ocasião dos Jogos Olímpicos de Verão de 1936, no exato local onde antes fora construído o Deutsche Stadion, planejado para os Jogos Olímpicos do ano de 1916. Recentemente o Olympiastadion foi completamente renovado e modernizado. A conservação e preservação de monumentos históricos foi um dos aspectos primordiais deste trabalho. Hoje o estádio além de ser um monumento histórico, em muito excede todas as exigências e expectativas impostas a um estádio moderno e internacional. Em momentos de tranquilidade e silêncio o estádio permite ao visitante contemplar a história recente e a arquitetura como arte.

WALTER KNOLL

SIGNAL IDUNA PARK
Dortmund | 2003
Planungsgruppe Schröder Schulte-Ladbeck Strothmann | Dortmund
Planungsgruppe Drahtler | Dortmund
Engels und Partner (SE) | Dortmund

Signal Iduna Park | Strobelallee 50 | 44139 Dortmund
www.westfalenstadion.de
Mainclub BVB Borussia Dortmund
Capacity: 82.900

Das Westfalenstadion wurde für die Fußballweltmeisterschaft 1974 errichtet und blieb bis Anfang der 1990er Jahre baulich nahezu unverändert. 1992 wurden auf der Nordtribüne befindliche Steh- in Sitzplätze umgerüstet, zwischen 1995 und 1999 wurden nacheinander die Tribünen aufgestockt. Eine letzte Ausbaustufe fand in der Sommerpause 2005 statt. Die Südtribüne bietet heute 25.000 Plätze und ist damit Europas größte Stehplatztribüne. Das neue 62 Meter hohe gelbe Pylonentragwerk ist markantes Ausrufezeichen am Fußballhimmel.

The Westfalenstadion ("Westphalia Stadium") was erected for the World Soccer Championships in 1974, and remain virtually unchanged until the early 90s. In 1992, the standing room on the north stands were converted into seating, and between 1995 and 1999, the stands were gradually augmented. One last remaining expansion phase took place during the summer break of 2005. The south stands now offer 25,000 seats, thus representing Europe‘s largest standing-room stands. The new, 62-meter high yellow pylon structure serves as a striking beacon in the soccer sky.

Le « Westfalenstadion » a été construit pour la Coupe du Monde de 1974 et n‘a subi pratiquement aucune modification jusqu‘au début des années 90. En 1992, les places debout dans la tribune nord ont cédé la place à une tribune de places assises puis, entre 1995 et 1999, les tribunes ont été surélevées. Les derniers aménagements ont été effectués pendant la trêve estivale de 2005. La tribune sud qui peut accueillir aujourd‘hui jusqu‘à 25 000 personnes est par conséquent la plus grande tribune de places debout d‘Europe. Les nouveaux piliers porteurs de 62 m de haut forment des points d‘exclamation bien visibles au firmament du football.

El Westfalenstadion (Estadio de Westfalia) se construyó para el Campeonato Mundial de Fútbol de 1974, y su estructura ha permanecido prácticamente inalterada hasta principios de los años noventa. En 1992 se remodelaron los asientos y las localidades de pie de la tribuna norte; entre 1995 y 1999 se ampliaron sucesivamente las diferentes tribunas. La última etapa de ampliación tuvo lugar en la pausa estival de 2005. La tribuna sur cuenta actualmente con 25.000 localidades, lo que la convierte en la tribuna de pie más grande de Europa. La nueva estructura portante de pilones de color amarillo y 62 metros de altura es el signo distintivo que se eleva hacia el cielo futbolístico.

Il Westfalenstadion fu eretto per il campionato mondiale di calcio del 1974 e rimase praticamente invariato fino all'inizio degli anni 90. Nel 1992 i posti in piedi sulla tribuna Nord furono trasformati in posti seduti; tra il 1995 e il 1999 le tribune furono ampliate una dopo l'altra. L'ultima fase d'ampliamento si svolse durante la pausa estiva del 2005. La tribuna Sud oggi offre 25.000 posti ed è quindi la tribuna con posti in piedi più grande d'Europa. La struttura portante a piloni gialli, alta 62 metri rappresenta un punto esclamativo rimarchevole nel cielo del calcio.

O Westfalenstadion foi contruído para a Copa do Mundo de Futebol de 1974 e até o início dos anos 90 pouca coisa foi alterada. Em 1992 arquibancadas e gerais na parte norte do estádio foram modernizadas, entre 1995 e 1999 as arquibancadas foram sendo ampliadas. Uma última fase de ampliação ocorreu no verão europeu de 2005. Hoje a arquibancada sul oferece 25.000 e tem a maior geral dos estádios europeus. O novo telhado amarelo de 62 metros de altura, sustentado por colunas, é mais uma formação marcante do futebol.

GoYellow
Wer Was Wo?
LANGNESE FAMILIENBLOCK
WARSTEINER
SIGNAL IDUNA
Coca-Cola
e-on

e·on e·on e·on e·on e·on e·on e·on e·on e·on e·on e·on
WARSTEINER
e·on e·on e·on
KNAUF INTERFER GRUPPE
KNAUF INTERFER GRUPPE

AIDA

AIDA LOUNGE
AIDA

COMMERZBANK ARENA
Frankfurt | 2005
gmp Architekten – von Gerkan, Mark und Partner | Hamburg
Schlaich Bergermann und Partner (SE) | Stuttgart
Krebs und Kiefer (SE) | Darmstadt

Commerzbank Arena | Mörfelder Landstraße 362 | 60528 Frankfurt
www.commerzbank-arena.de
Mainclub: Eintracht Frankfurt
Capacity: 52.000

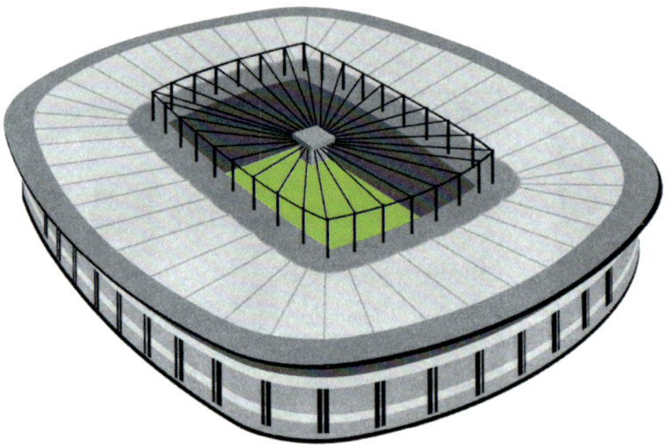

Die strenge Rhythmik der Gesamtkonstruktion wird durch 30 Meter hohe Stützsäulen geprägt. Im Abstand von je 16 Metern geben sie dem ovalen Bau ein wenig vom wuchtigen Aussehen eines Colosseums. Nach dem Umbau präsentiert sich das Stadion mit einer absolut innovativen Zeltdach-Konstruktion, die sich in nur wenigen Minuten über dem Spielfeld auseinander und zusammenfalten lässt und in einem Videowürfel verschwindet. Somit verwandelt sich das verschließbare Dach in das größte Cabrio der Welt.

The strict rhythm of the overall construction is characterized by its 30-meter high support beams. Spaced at intervals of 16 meters, they lend the oval structure of the former Waldstadion ("Forest Stadium") Frankfurt the somewhat bulky look of a coliseum. After the renovation work, the stadium now sports an absolutely innovative tent-roof construction which can be unfolded over the playing field and folded up in a matter of minutes, disappearing into a video cube. Thus, the closable roof transforms the venue into the largest convertible in the world.

La conception sévère de l'ensemble de la construction est dominée par des piliers de support de 30 m de haut. Installés tous les 16 m, ils donnent à la construction ovale de l'ancien Waldstadion de Francfort un peu l'apparence massive d'un colisée. Après les travaux d'aménagement, le stade possède désormais une toiture pliante très sophistiquée qui peut être dépliée et repliée au-dessus du terrain en l'espace de quelques minutes et disparaître dans un cube vidéo. Le toit rétractable devient ainsi la plus grande décapotable du monde.

Las columnas de soporte de 30 metros de altura le imprimen su carácter especial a la rígida rítmica de la obra global. Estas columnas, erigidas a una distancia de 16 metros, respectivamente, confieren a la construcción oval del antiguo Waldstadion Frankfurt (Estadio Forestal de Francfort) la apariencia majestuosa de un coloseo. Tras su reconstrucción, el estadio se presenta hoy con un techo de pabellón absolutamente innovador, que en pocos minutos se despliega encima del terreno de juego y luego se vuelve a replegar, desapareciendo en un cubo de vídeo. De esta forma, el techo cerrable se convierte en el descapotable más grande del mundo.

L'austera ritmica dell'insieme costruttivo è caratterizzata dai piloni di supporto alti 30 metri. Con l'interasse di 16 metri tra loro, i piloni danno alla costruzione ovale del vecchio Waldstadion Frankfurt un poco dell'aspetto imponente del Colosseo. Dopo la ricostruzione, lo stadio si presenta con un tetto a padiglione assolutamente innovativo che si stende e si ripiega in pochi minuti sopra il campo di gioco, scomparendo in un cubo con pareti a schermi video. Così il tetto apribile si trasforma nella decappottabile più grande del mondo.

Colunas de 30 metros de altura dão a esta construção o aspecto grave que a caracteriza. Com um espaçamento de 16 metros elas envolvem toda a construção oval do então Waldstadion Frankfurt, dando ao estádio um ar de Colosseu. Com a reconstrução o estádio ganhou um telhado especial, que em alguns poucos minutos pode ser aberto ou fechado, "desaparecendo" em um dado de vídeo. Assim, este estádio com seu telhado conversível pode transformar-se no maior cabriolé do mundo.

FRANKFURT

COMMERZBANK ARENA

COMMERZBANK ARENA

VELTINS ARENA
Gelsenkirchen | 2001
HPP Hentrich-Petschnigg & Partner | Düsseldorf
Pelle Ingenieurbüro für Bauwesen (SE) | Dortmund

Veltins Arena | Ernst-Kuzorra-Weg 1 | 45891 Gelsenkirchen
www.veltins-arena.de
Mainclub: FC Schalke 04
Capacity: 61.500

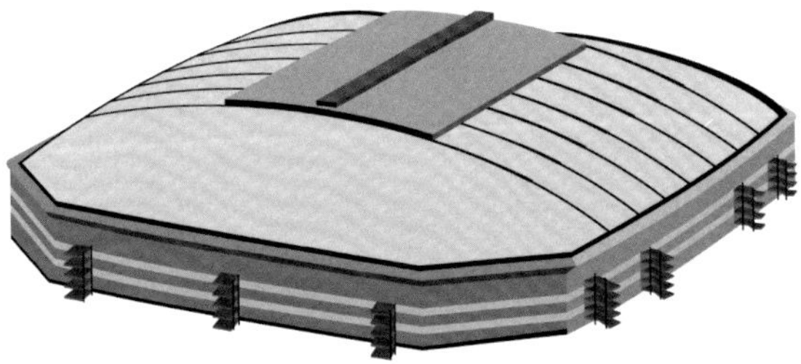

HILIPS
Th 10
Block 53-58
Ost Tribüne
U
T

Die technische Ausstattung des wohl modernsten Stadion Europas ist richtungsweisend für den Stadionbau. Das Stadion kann mittels eines verschließbaren Daches bei Bedarf in eine Halle umgewandelt werden. In der Zeit zwischen den Fußballspielen wird der Spielfeldrasen mittels einer Hydraulik aus der Arena heraus geschoben. Zu diesem Zweck wurde die Südtribüne freischwebend wie eine Brücke über dem Durchlass gebaut. Das Stadion ist mit einer Kapelle ausgestattet, in der regelmäßig Taufen und Hochzeiten stattfinden.

The technical equipment of the former Schalke Arena, probably the most modern stadium in Europe, is trend-setting for stadium construction. The stadium can be transformed into a hall with its closable roof. In the periods between soccer games, the playing field turf is pushed out of the arena with a hydraulic mechanism. That is why the south stands were built like a bridge, “floating” over the opening. The stadium is also equipped with a chapel, in which baptisms and weddings regularly take place.

L‘équipement technique de l‘ancienne « Arena auf Schalke », le stade le plus moderne d‘Europe, est devenu une nouvelle référence en matière de construction de stades. Cette arène est en mesure, grâce à son toit rétractable, de se transformer en salle de concerts ou de compétition si besoin est. Entre les matchs de foot, la pelouse amovible disparaît du terrain au moyen de dispositifs hydrauliques. Dans ce but, la tribune sud flotte comme un pont au-dessus du passage. Le stade est doté d‘une chapelle dans laquelle se déroulent régulièrement baptêmes et mariages.

El equipamiento técnico de la antigua Arena auf Schalke, propablemente el estadio más moderno de Europa, es el modelo a seguir en la construcción de estadios. Gracias a su techo cerrable, el estadio se puede utilizar, en su caso, como pabellón. En los espacios de tiempo entre los diferentes partidos de fútbol, el césped se retira del terreno de la arena con ayuda de un sistema hidráulico. Para ello, se ha construido la tribuna sur en forma suspendida, a modo de puente, por encima de la zona de acceso. El estadio dispone de una capilla en la que se celebran regularmente bautizos y bodas.

L'equipaggiamento tecnico dell'ex Arena auf Schalke che è probabilmente lo stadio più moderno d'Europa, è orientativo per la costruzione di stadi. Grazie ad un tetto apribile, lo stadio si lascia trasformare in un padiglione. Nei periodi tra le partite, il campo da gioco si lascia spingere fuori dell'Arena per mezzo di un impianto idraulico. A tale scopo la tribuna Sud fu costruita sospesa in aria, come un ponte sopra il passaggio. Lo stadio dispone di una cappella ove si celebrano regolarmente battezzi e matrimoni.

O equipamento técnico do estádio conhecido como Arena auf Schalke, provavelmente o mais moderno da Europa, é uma visão do futuro. Um telhado conversível transforma o estádio em um enorme ginásio, caso necessário. Nos intervalos dos jogos uma instalação hidráulica retira o gramado do Arena. Para tanto, a arquibancada sul foi construída como uma ponte. O estádio dispõe de uma capela onde são regularmente realizados batizados e casamentos.

14

S2
S3

FC SCHALKE 04
VELTINS
adidas
VICTORIA

MAXDATA
FC SCHALKE 04
VELTINS
VICTORIA
airberlin.com

VICTORIA
VICTORIA
VELTINS
erdgas
VICTORIA

VELTINS
J.W. OSTENDORF
STADA Arzneimittel
adidas
ITEC

VELTINS

VELTINS

WC
HERREN
ATACAMA

AOL Arena
Hamburg | 2000
MOS Architekten | Hamburg
Schlaich Bergermann und Partner (SE) | Stuttgart

AOL Arena | Millerntorplatz 1 | 20359 Hamburg
www.aol-arena.de
Mainclub: HSV Hamburger Sport-Verein e.V
Capacity: 55.000

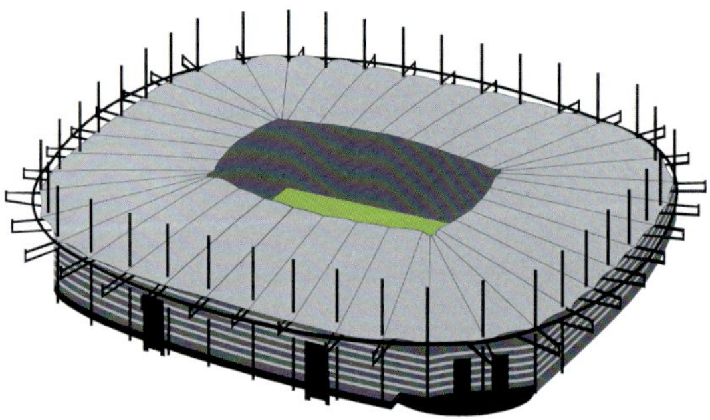

AOL ARENA

1953 wurde es auf Trümmerschutt wiedererrichtet; das Volksparkstadion war Austragungsort zahlreicher weiterer Länderspiele. Seit März 1988 hatte man die Anlagen des alten Volksparkstadions in vier Abschnitten abgerissen, dann das Spielfeld gedreht und die Tribünenseiten neu aufgebaut. Die Dachkonstruktion aus einer weißen, transluzenten Membran sorgt für gleichmäßige Helligkeit und lässt eine auf das Spielfeld bezogene rechteckige Öffnung im Dach.

In 1953, it was rebuilt atop a pile of debris; the "Volksparkstadion" was the site of a number of national games. Starting in March of 1988, the old Volksparkstadion was torn down in four segments. The playing field was then rotated and the surrounding stands rebuilt. The roof construction, consisting of a white, translucent membrane, ensures uniform brightness and allows a rectangular opening in the roof over the playing field.

Construit en 1953 sur les décombres, le « Volksparkstadion » a accueilli de nombreuses rencontres nationales. En mars 1988, les travaux débutent avec la démolition des équipements en quatre phases, la rotation de la pelouse et la reconstruction des tribunes. La toiture composée d'une membrane blanche et translucide permet un éclairage homogène et laisse une ouverture rectangulaire juste au-dessus de l'aire de jeu.

El Volksparkstadion, reconstruido en 1953 sobre los escombros de guerra, fue lugar de celebración de numerosos partidos internacionales. En marzo de 1988 se empezaron a demoler las instalaciones del antiguo Volksparkstadion en cuatro etapas; a continuación se giró el terreno de juego y se reconstruyeron los lados de las tribunas. El techo consta de una membrana blanca translúcida que aporta una luminosidad homogéna al estadio, con una apertura rectangular que hace referencia al terreno de juego.

Nel 1953 il Volksparkstadion fu ricostruito sulle macerie; numerose partite internazionali vi furono disputate. Iniziando a marzo del 1988, gli impianti del vecchio Volksparkstadion furono abbattuti in quattro sezioni, il campo da gioco fu girato e le tribune furono ricostruite. La costruzione del tetto, composta di una membrana bianca e traslucida provvede ad un'omogenea luminosità e lascia uno spazio rettangolare nel tetto che rispecchia le dimensioni del campo di gioco.

Em 1953 o Volksparkstadion foi reconstruído a partir de escombros e nele foram realizadas um sem-número de partidas internacionais. Em março de 1988 as instalações do antigo Volksparkstadion foram desmontadas em quatro secções, em seguida o campo foi girado e as arquibancadas foram reconstruídas. A construção do telhado, feita num material branco e transluzente que lembra uma membrana, oferece luz uniforme e tem uma abertura retangular sobre o gramado.

ADIG
ADIG
Eingang

E2

Wir kennen jede Kurve!
simply worldwide BIRKART GLOBISTICS
AOLARENA
RADIO HAMBURG
ADIG
AOL
CASIO CASIO
DIGITAL
puma

LLOYD FONDS
NORDCAPITAL
Sysmex
Deutsche Bank

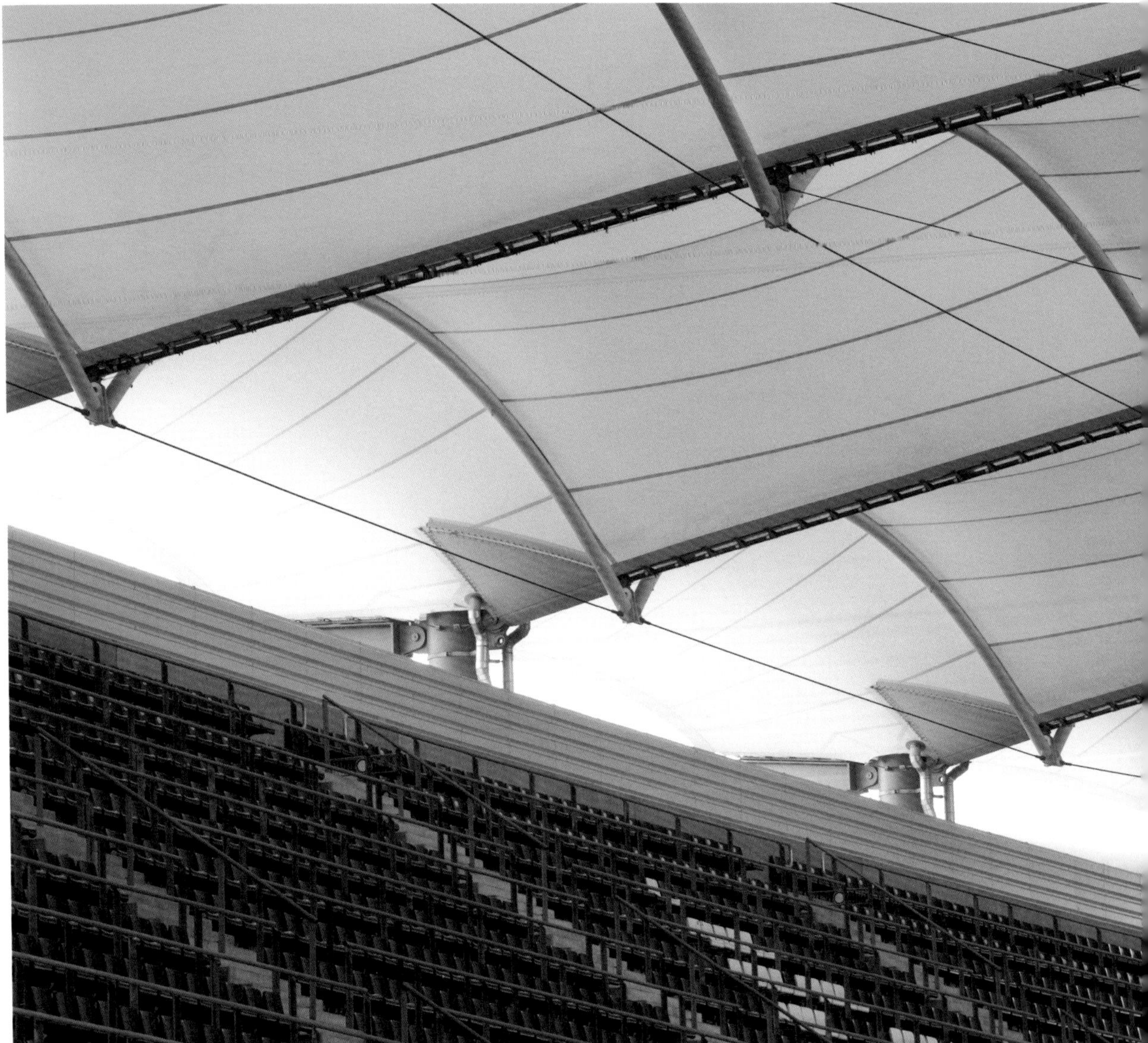

Snacks & Getränke
Getränke Express
15,16
Ausgang

Nord
Loge
23-36

Erfrischung gefällig ?
HOLSTEN
HOLSTEN

PUMA

HSV
PUMA

H S V
KART GLOBISTICS
SIGNAL IDUNA
RADIO HAMBURG

RADIO HAMBURG
www. hsv. de

BIRKART
www.birkart.com
AOLARENA
MOPO. So ist das.
www.mopo.de
Fussi? HSV! Auto?
AUTOLEASING

AWD-ARENA
Hannover | 2004
Schulitz + Partner Architekten BDA | Braunschweig
RFR Ingénieurs (SE) | Paris Stuttgart

AWD Arena | Arthur-Menge-Ufer 5 | 30169 Hannover
www.awd-arena.de
Mainclub: Hannover 96
Capacity: 53.000

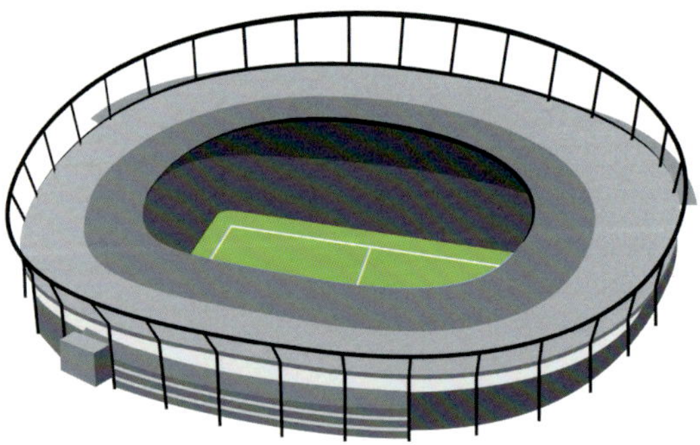

AWDarena
96
AWDarena

Geschichtlich gesehen ist das Hannover Stadion einen enorme Bauleistung der Nachkriegszeit. Altes mit dem neuem verbinden war somit die größte Herausforderung des aktuellen Stadionumbaues. Die niedrigen Standards von 1954 mussten mit den heutigen Komfortansprüchen in Einklang gebracht werden. Mit dem opaken Dach für den Oberrang und einem Dach aus ETFE-Folie für den Unterrang überdecken zwei unterschiedliche Dächer das Stadion.

Historically speaking, the former Niedersachsenstadion ("Lower Saxony Stadium") is an enormous architectural achievement of the post-war period. Fusing the old with the new was thus the greatest challenge for the new stadium renovation. The low standards of 1954 needed to be updated to conform to modern demands for comfort. The stadium sports two different roofs: an opaque roof for the upper tier and a roof made of ETFE foil for the lower tier.

D'un point de vue historique, l'ancien « Niedersachsenstadion » est une énorme prouesse architecturale de l'après-guerre. Le principal défi des travaux de transformation actuels du stade a ainsi consisté à faire du neuf avec de l'ancien. Les normes peu exigeantes de 1954 ont dû être adaptées aux critères actuels en matière de confort. Avec la toiture opaque pour les gradins supérieurs et une toiture en panneaux de ETFE (éthylène tétrafluo-éthylène) pour les gradins inférieurs, le stade est couvert de deux toits différents.

Desde el punto de vista histórico, el antiguo Niedersachsenstadion (Estadio de la Baja Sajonia) representa una enorme obra de construcción de la época de posguerra. El combinar lo viejo con lo nuevo fue, pues, el mayor desafío del actual estadio. Los bajos estándares de calidad de 1954 se han tenido que adaptar a las exigencias de comodidad actuales. Hoy, el estadio está cubierto por dos techos diferentes: el techo opaco para la grada superior y un techo de paneles de ETFE para la granda inferior.

Dal punto di vista storico il vecchio Niedersachsenstadion rappresentò un'enorme prestazione architettonica del post-guerra. Abbinare il vecchio al nuovo pertanto costituì la maggiore sfida dell'attuale ricostruzione dello stadio. I bassi standard del 1954 andarono fatte concordare con le esigenze odierne di confort. Con il tetto opaco per le balconate superiori ed un tetto fatto di pellicola ETFE per le balconate inferiori, due tetti differenti coprono lo stadio.

Sob o ponto de vista histórico, a construção do então Niedersachsenstadion é um feito memorável do pós-guerra. Assim, o grande desafio na renovação deste estádio foi preservar o velho e introduzir o novo. A divisa era harmonizar as exigências modernas com os padrões de 1954, que pouco condizem com os atuais. O telhado foi construído em dois materiais diferentes: a arquibancada superior é coberta com um telhado opaco, enquanto a arquibancada inferior é coberta com uma membrana de ETFE.

Viel Spaß in der
AWD arena
AWD

Viel Spaß in der
AWDarena
Die Roten
AWD

Continental
Continental
TUI.de
AWD
Ihr unabhängiger Finanzoptimierer

nanzoptimierer AWD
TUI

HAVANNA LOUNGE
BUSINESS CLUB
Gilde Brauerei
hängiger Finanzoptimierer
AWD
Offensivtaktik für mehr Geld
AWD
Ihr unabhängiger Finanzoptimierer
TUI
TUI
TUI
TUI
TUI

Neue Presse
TUI
TUI
TUI
TUI
TUI
TUI

96
Die Roten
96
Die Roten
96
Die Roten

FRITZ-WALTER-STADION
Kaiserslautern | 2006
Fiebiger GmbH Architekten + Ingenieure | Kaiserslautern
WZ Ingenieure (SE) | Kaiserslautern
KHP Konig, Heunisch und Partner (SE) | Frankfurt

Fritz-Walter-Stadion | Fritz-Walter-Straße 1 | 67663 Kaiserslautern
www.fck.de
Mainclub: 1 FC Kaiserslautern
Capacity: 48.500

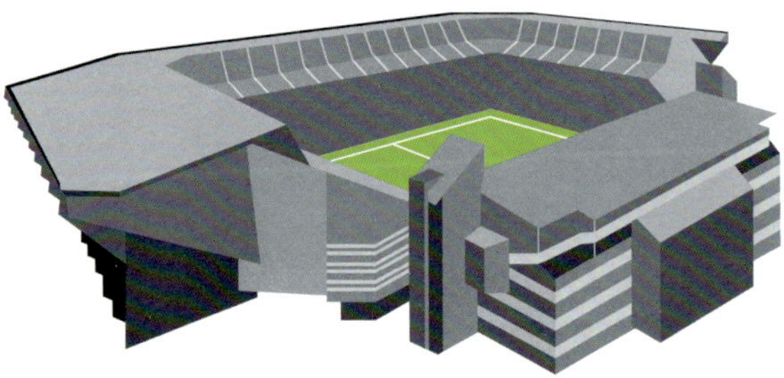

Das Stadion ist im Jahr 1920 auf dem Betzenberg erbaut worden. Seit 1985 trägt es den Namen von Fritz Walter, mit dem der 1. FCK in den Jahren 1951 und 1953 erstmals Deutscher Meister wurde. Das Stadion ist ein in sich geschlossener Kubus und hat als Besonderheit die in den Ecken an beiden Seiten der Nordtribüne angeordneten Türme.

The stadium was built in the year 1920 on Betzenberg Mountain. Since 1985, it has borne the name of Fritz Walter, with whom the 1st FC Kaiserslautern won their first German Championships in the years 1951 and 1953. The stadium is a closed cube, whose special features are the towers situated in the corners on both sides of the north stands.

Le stade a été construit en 1920 sur le Betzenberg et porte, depuis 1985, le nom de Fritz Walter avec qui le club 1. FCK a été sacré champion d'Allemagne pour la première fois en 1951 puis en 1953. Le stade est un cube fermé avec une particularité, à savoir les tours qui occupent les angles nord de l'enceinte des deux côtés de la tribune.

El estadio fue construido en 1920 sobre el Betzenberg. Desde 1985 porta el nombre de Fritz Walter, con quien el 1. FCK se convirtió en los años 1951 y 1953 por primera vez en Campeón alemán. Este estadio es un cubo cerrado, cuya particularidad son las torres ubicadas en las esquinas de los dos lados de la tribuna norte.

Lo stadio fu costruito nel 1920 sul Betzenberg. Dal 1985 porta il nome di Fritz Walter con il quale il 1. FCK divenne per la prima volta campione nazionale negli anni 1951 e 1953. Lo stadio è un cubo chiuso e come sua particolarità è disposta di torri nei due angoli della tribuna Nord.

O estádio foi construído do ano de 1920 no Betzenberg. Desde 1985 o estádio porta o nome de Fritz Walter, jogador do 1. FCK nos anos de 1951 e 1953, quando o clube sagrou-se campeão alemão pela primeira vez. O estádio é um cubo fechado em si, cuja característica peculiar são as torres existentes nos cantos da arquibancada norte.

1. FC
FRITZ-WALT
BAUHAUS
Deutsche Vermögensberatung
ODDSET
Deutsche Vermögensberatung
WÜRTH

DIGITAL
DIGITAL
Deutsche
Vermögensberatung
Kabel Deutschland

Zwei starke Partner!

18

Deutsche
Vermögensberatung
Block
M/N
Reihe
21-30
Aufgang
8.1

Block
L/M
K/L

RHEIN-ENERGIE-STADION
Köln | 2004
gmp Architekten – von Gerkan, Mark und Partner | Hamburg
Schlaich Bergermann und Partner (SE) | Stuttgart

RheinEnergieStadion | Aachener Straße 999 | 50933 Köln
www.rheinenergiestadion.de
Mainclubs: 1 FC Köln
Capacity: 51.000

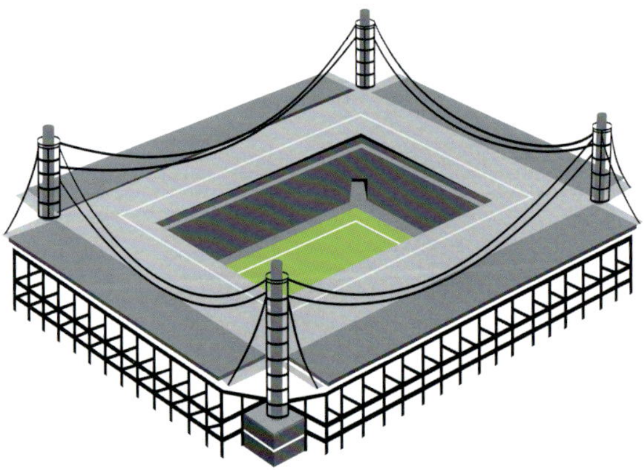

Tribüne West

Das RheinEnergieStadion ist eine Konzert- und Wettkampfstätte in Köln. Sein Vorläufer ist das 1923 an gleicher Stelle erbaute Müngersdorfer Stadion, welches 1975 neu errichtet wurde. Gegenüber dem alten Stadion hat die neue Arena wesentlich an Atmosphäre gewonnen. Architektonisch bestechen die vier hohen Masten, die das Dach tragen. Nähert man sich der Rhein-Metropole, so bilden die vier erleuchteten Pylonen ein deutliches Signal.

The RheinEnergieStadion is a concert and sports venue in Cologne. Its predecessor was the Müngersdorfer Stadium, built on the same site in 1923 and renovated in 1975. The new arena has gained considerably with regard to atmosphere in comparison with the old one. From the architectural standpoint, the four high masts bearing the roof are eye-catchers. Approaching the city of Cologne, one sees the four illuminated pylons as the new landmark of this metropolis on the Rhine.

Le « RheinEnergieStadion » à Cologne accueille concerts et compétitions. Son prédécesseur est le „Müngersdorfer Stadion“ construit en 1923 sur ce même emplacement puis reconstruit en 1975. En face de l‘ancien stade, la nouvelle arène a nettement gagné en ambiance. D‘un point de vue architectonique, les quatre hauts mâts qui soutiennent le toit constituent une particularité. Les visiteurs arrivant dans la métropole rhénane ne peuvent pas manquer les quatre tours éclairées qui forment le nouvel emblème de la ville de Cologne.

El RheinEnergieStadion es un pabellón para conciertos y certámenes situado en la ciudad de Colonia. Su predecesor fue el Müngersdorfer Stadion (Estadio de Müngersdorf) erigido en 1923 en el mismo lugar y reconstruido en 1975. Comparado con el antiguo estadio, la nueva arena posee mucho más ambiente. Desde el punto de vista arquitectónico destacan los cuatro postes de gran altitud que soportan el techo. Cuando uno se acerca a la metrópoli a orillas del Rin, los cuatro pilones iluminados destacan como el nuevo símbolo emblemático de Colonia.

Il RheinEnergieStadion è fatto per concerti e manifestazioni sportive da tenersi a Cologna. Suo precursore è il Müngersdorfer Stadion che fu eretto nel 1923 nello stesso luogo, ricostruito poi nel 1975. Nei confronti con il vecchio stadio, la nuova arena ha guadagnato notevolmente d’atmosfera. Dal punto di vista architettonico sono rimarchevoli i quattro piloni alti che reggono il tetto. Avvicinandosi alla metropoli sul Reno, i quattro piloni illuminati formano il nuovo emblema della città di Cologna.

O RheinEnergieStadion é utilizado para a eventos desportivos e musicais na cidade de Colônia. Este estádio foi construído em 1975, no mesmo local onde em 1923 havia sido construído o estádio Müngersdorfer. Frente ao antigo estádio, esta nova arena tem muito mais personalidade e os quatro mastros que suportam o telhado são sua característica arquitetônica mais marcante. Iluminados eles podem ser vistos já de longe por aqueles que se aproximam desta metrópole às margens do Reno, e são um novo símbolo de Colônia.

Rhein
Energie
GEW RheinEnergie
Stadion

Rhein
RheinEnergieStadion
GERLING
HIT
BAUHAUS
funny-frisch

ergie
Jack Wolfskin
RheinEnergieStadion

W13
Tribüne West
RheinEnergieStadion

ffel Kölsch
RheinEnergieStadion
GERLING
WM-Countdown präsentiert von
284 02:19:73
HIT
WO GUT LEBEN WENIG KOSTET
ZEG

Jack Wolfskin
RheinEnergieStadion
RheinEnergie

1. FC Köln

ZENTRALSTADION

Leipzig | 2004
ARGE Zentralstadion Leipzig: Wirth + Wirth Architects | Basel
Glöckner Architekten | Nürnberg
Körber, Barton, Fahle | Freiburg
Peter A. Kugler und Partner (SE) | Munich
IPL Ingenieure für Tragwerk und Leichtbau (SE) | Radolfzell

Zentralstadion Leipzig | Am Sportforum 3 | 04105 Leipzig
www.sportforum-leipzig.com/zentralstadion
Mainclubs: FC Sachsen Leipzig
Capacity: 45.000

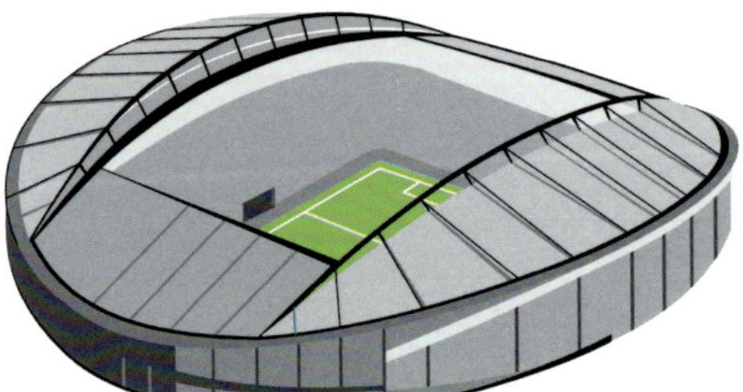

Das Zentralstadion wurde 1956 aus dem Kriegsschutt der Stadt erbaut. Damals hatte es eine Kapazität von 100.000 Zuschauern weswegen es auch den Beinamen „Stadion der Hunderttausend“ erhielt. 1997 beschloss die Stadt Leipzig, innerhalb des alten Stadionwalls ein neues, reines Fußballstadion zu bauen. Über Brücken, die das neue Stadion mit dem alten Stadionwall verbinden, gelangen die Besucher zu den Sitzplätzen auf den umlaufenden Rängen. Mit dem Zentralstadion verfügt Leipzig über eines der architektonisch und technisch modernsten Stadien der Welt.

The Zentralstadion (“Central Stadium”) was constructed out of war debris from the city in 1956. At the time, it had a capacity of 100,000 spectators, which earned it the nickname “Stadium of the Hundred Thousand”. In 1997, the city of Leipzig decided to erect a new stadium solely for soccer inside the walls of the old stadium. Visitors access seating in the tiers surrounding the field over bridges that connect the new stadium with the old stadium wall. In the Zentralstadion, Leipzig possesses one of the most architecturally and technically modern stadiums in the world.

Le « Zentralstadion » a été construit en 1956 sur les ruines laissées par la guerre dans la ville. A l‘époque, il pouvait accueillir 100 000 spectateurs d‘où le surnom de « stade des cent-mille ». En 1997, la ville de Leipzig décide d‘ériger un nouveau stade dédié uniquement au football dans l‘ancienne enceinte. La nouvelle structure et les vestiges du passé sont reliés par des passerelles, qui guident les spectateurs vers leurs places couvertes, sur les deux étages de l‘ovale. Avec le « Zentralstadion », Leipzig possède aujourd‘hui l‘un des stades les plus modernes du monde au point de vue architectonique et technique.

El Zentralstadion (Estadio Central) se construyó en el año 1956 con los escombros de los edificios destruidos en la guerra. En aquella época tenía una capacidad de 100.000 espectadores, por lo que obtuvo el sobrenombre de “Estadio de los cien mil”. En 1997, la ciudad de Leipzig decidió construir un nuevo terreno de juego dedicado exclusivamente al fútbol dentro del antiguo terraplén del estadio. Los visitantes acceden -a través de los puentes que unen el nuevo estadio con el antiguo terraplén del estadio- hasta las localidades situadas en las gradas circulares. Con el Zentralstadion, Leipzig posee uno de los estadios más modernos del mundo desde el punto de vista técnico y arquitectónico.

Lo Zentralstadion fu costruito nel 1956 sulle macerie di guerra della città. All'epoca aveva una capacità di 100.000 spettatori ed ottenne quindi il soprannome dello "stadio dei centomila". Nel 1997 il comune di Lipsia decise di costruire all'interno dei muri dello stadio un nuovo stadio dedicato esclusivamente al calcio. Attraverso i ponti che collegano il nuovo stadio con il vallo del vecchio stadio, gli spettatori raggiungono i posti seduti delle balconate disposte in circolare. Con lo Zentralstadion, Lipsia dispone di uno degli stadi più moderni al mondo a livello architettonico e tecnico.

O Zentralstadion foi construído 1956 com os escombros que a guerra deixou na cidade. À época tinha capacidade para 100.000 visitantes, o que lhe rendeu o apelido de "estádio dos cem mil". Em 1997 a cidade de Leipzig decidiu construir um novo estádio, exclusivamente para o futebol, dentro das demarcações do velho estádio. Pontes vencem o antigo fosso e conduzem os visitantes ao interior do estádio. O Zentralstadion em Leipzig é um dos mais modernos do mundo, tanto em termos arquitectônicos, quanto técnicos.

C D
A
B A
B C D

Erdgas fahren
Clever sparen
Stadtwerke Leipzig
Stadtwerke Leipzig
erdga

Wasser zum Leben
erdgas

erdgas
KUPPER
erdgas

ALLIANZ ARENA

Munich | 2004
Herzog und de Meuron | Basel
Ove Arup & Partners (SE) | Berlin
IPL Ingenieure für Tragwerk und Leichtbau (SE) | Radolfzell
Sailer Stepan und Partner (SE) | Munich

Allianz Arena München | Werner-Heisenberg-Allee 25 | 80939 München
www.allianz-arena.de
Mainclubs: FC Bayern München | TSV 1860 München
Capacity: 66.000 Plätze

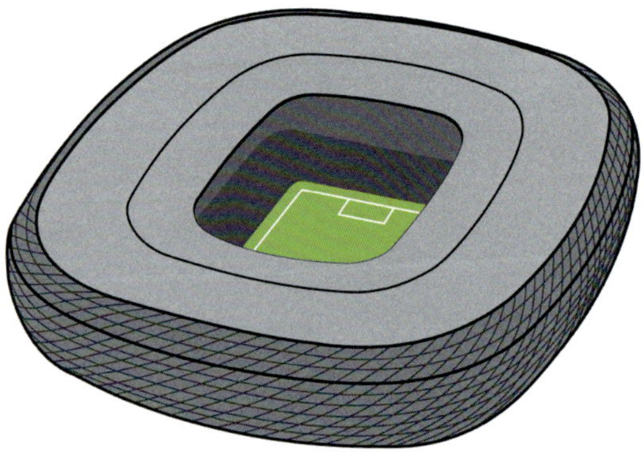

Allianz

Die Arena zählt aufgrund ihrer Außenhülle zu den ungewöhnlichsten und optisch reizvollsten Stadien der Welt. Die glatte Fassade aus einer rautenförmigen Umhüllung, die sich über Projektionen in unterschiedliche Farbenspiele tauchen lässt, gibt dem Gebäude eine magische Poesie. Die spektakulär ausschauende Fassade besteht aus 2.874 EFTE-Folienkissen. Jedes Kissen kann separat in Weiß oder mit Blau oder Rot in der Farbe der jeweils spielenden Heimmannschaft erstrahlen.

The outer shell of the Allianz Arena makes it one of the most unusual and visually attractive stadiums in the world. The smooth façade of the outer shell, whose surface possesses a diamond-shaped pattern, enables various color schemes to be projected onto it, lending a magical poetry to the structure. This visually spectacular façade consists of 2,874 EFTE foil pillows. Each pillow can be illuminated separately in white or glow in blue or red in the colors of the respective home team.

L'« Allianz Arena » présente un aspect extérieur vraiment unique qui en fait l'un des stades les plus inhabituels et spectaculaires du monde. La façade lisse constituée de grands panneaux en forme de losange projette sur la structure un kaléidoscope bariolé qui donne à l'édifice un rayonnement magique. La façade d'apparence spectaculaire est composée de 2 874 panneaux de EFTE (éthylène tétrafluo-éthylène). Chaque panneau peut être éclairé individuellement en blanc, en bleu ou en rouge dans la couleur de l'équipe qui joue à domicile.

Debido a su cubierta exterior, la Allianz Arena es uno de los estadios más singulares y de mayor atractivo óptico del mundo. Su fachada lisa compuesta por una cubierta en forma de rombo, que al proyectarse luz sobre ella se sume en un mar de colores, confiere al edificio una magia poética. La espectacular fachada consta de 2.874 paneles de EFTE. Cada uno de estos paneles puede iluminarse por separado en blanco o en azul y rojo de forma correspondiente al color del equipo local que esté jugando.

L'Allianz Arena con il suo involucro esterno conta tra gli stadi più inconsueti ed otticamente attraenti del mondo. La facciata liscia fatta di un involucro a forma di rombo che s'immerge in diversi giochi di luci grazie ad un sistema di proiezioni, dà all'edificio una poesia magica. La facciata dall'aspetto spettacolare consiste in 2.874 cuscini di pellicola EFTE. Ogni cuscino può illuminarsi separatamente in bianco oppure con il blu ed il rosso nei colori delle squadre giocando in casa.

O aspecto externo do Allianz Arena faz deste estádio um dos mais inusitados e interessantes do mundo. A fachada lisa, formada por muitos losângulos, pode ser iluminada em cores fascinantes, dando a esta construção um aspecto mágico. No total a fachada tem 2.874 “travesseiros” em folha EFTE e cada um deles pode ser iluminado individualmente em branco, azul ou vermelho, conforme a cor do time que alí joga.

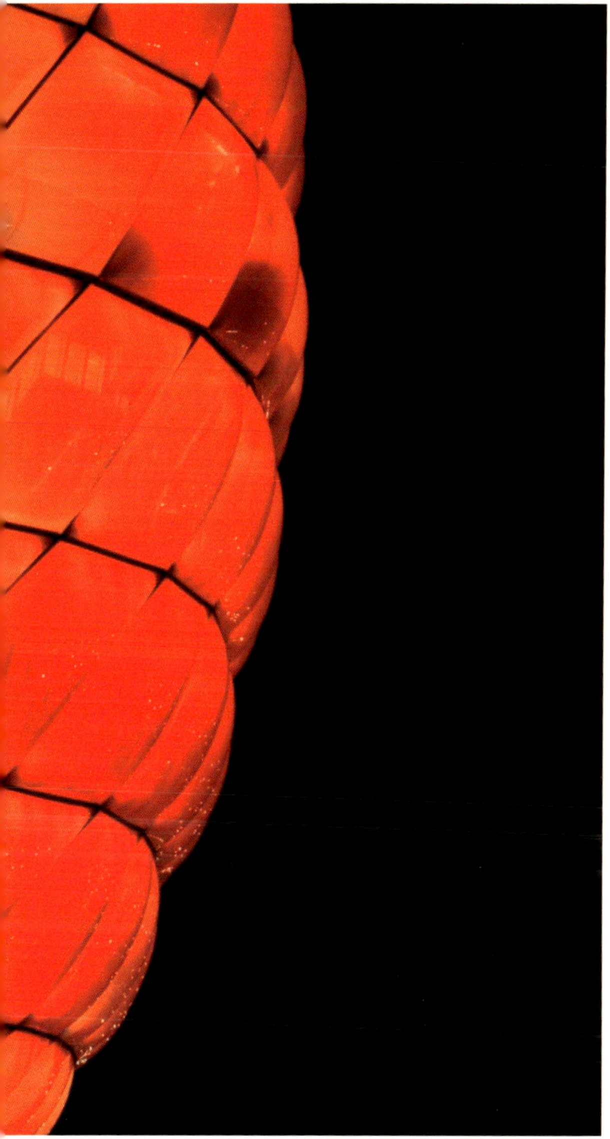

12
11
10

Allianz Arena

Allianz Arena

Allianz Arena

FRANKEN-STADION
Nürnberg | 2005
HPP Hentrich-Petschnigg & Partner | Düsseldorf
Ingenieurbüro Köhler + Seitz (SE) | Nürnberg

Frankenstadion Nürnberg | Max-Morlock-Platz 1 | 90471 Nürnberg
www.franken-stadion.de
Mainclub: 1. FC Nürnberg
Capacity: 44 308 Plätze

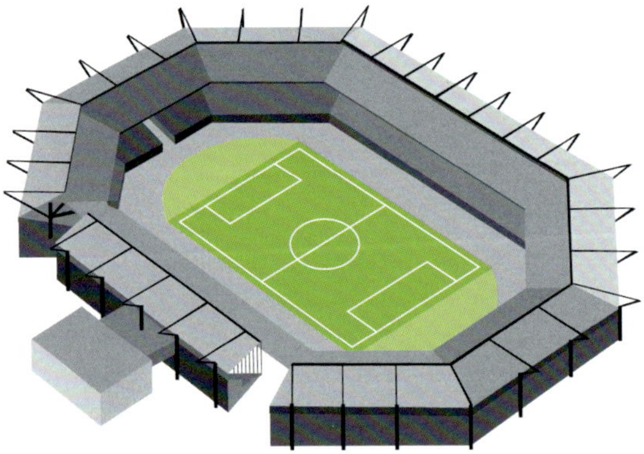

Die Sportarena weist bereits eine fast 80-jährige Geschichte auf. 1928 war das „Städtische Stadion“ entstanden, damals mit einem Fassungsvermögen von 50.000 Zuschauern. Nachdem der 1. FC Nürnberg 1961 zum achten Mal deutscher Fußballmeister geworden war, entschloss sich die Stadt zur Einführung der Bundesliga das Stadion umzubauen. Ab 1987 folgte eine Generalsanierung und Renovierung, 1991 wurde das Stadion als Franken-Stadion eingeweiht.

This sporting arena boasts an almost 80-year history. In 1928, the Städtisches Stadion ("City Stadium") was erected, at the time with a capacity of 50,000 spectators. After the 1st FC Nuremberg had become the German champions for the eighth time in 1961, the city decided to renovate the stadium for the introduction of the Bundesliga. Starting in 1987, a general refurbishment and renovation took place. In 1991, the stadium was inaugurated as the Franken-Stadion ("Franconia Stadium").

La « Sportarena » existe depuis déjà presque 80 ans. Le « stade municipal » a été construit en 1928 et pouvait accueillir à l'époque 50 000 spectateurs. Suite au huitième sacre national du 1. FC Nuremberg en 1961, la ville décide de reconstruire le terrain à temps pour la première saison de la Bundesliga. A partir de 1987, le stade est rénové de fond en comble et modernisé. En 1991, le « Franken-Stadion » est alors inauguré.

La Sportarena cuenta con una historia de casi ochenta años. En 1928 se inauguró el Städtische Stadion (Estadio Municipal), que en aquellos entonces contaba con una capacidad de 50.000 espectadores. Después de que en 1961 el 1. FC Nürnberg se convirtiera por octava vez en campeón nacional de fútbol, la ciudad decidió remodelar el estadio con motivo de la introducción de la Bundesliga. A partir de 1987 tuvo lugar el saneamiento general y la renovación del estadio, que se inauguró finalmente en 1991 bajo el nombre de Franken-Stadion.

La Sportarena ha una storia quasi ottantenne. Nel 1928 fu eretto lo "Städtische Stadion", con una capacità all'epoca di 50.000 spettatori. Dopo che il 1. FC Nürnberg nel 1961 divenne campione nazionale per l'ottava volta il comune decise di trasformare lo stadio, all'occasione dell'introduzione della lega nazionale di calcio. A partire dal 1987 fu eseguito un risanamento e rinnovamento generale; nel 1991 lo stadio fu inaugurato come Franken-Stadion.

O estádio Sportarena já tem quase 80 anos. Em 1928 foi constuído o "estádio municipal", com capacidade para 50.000 espectadores. Depois que o 1. FC Nürnberg conquistou pela oitava vez o título de campeão alemão, em 1961, e com a fundação da Bundesliga, a cidade decidiu renovar o estádio. A partir de 1987 ele foi completamente saneado e renovado, e em 1991 o estádio foi inaugurado como Franken-Stadion.

6
5a

Coca-Cola
mister+lady★jeans
NÜRN
mister+lady★jeans
Coca-Cola
ARO
ARO

mister+lady★jeans★
REHAU Partner am Bau
Coca-Cola
Coca-Cola
GERSTÄCKER

Coca-Cola
Coca-Cola
Coca-Cola

mister+lady★jeans★
mister+lady★jeans★
Tucher
Tucher
Coca-Cola
Coca-Cola
Block 15h

GOTTLIEB-DAIMLER-STADION

Stuttgart | 2005

Schlaich Bergermann & Partner | Stuttgart

Architekten Arat-Siegel & Partner | Stuttgart

Weideplan | Stuttgart

Gottlieb-Daimler-Stadion | Mercedesstraße 87 | 70372 Stuttgart

www.gottlieb-daimler-stadion.de

Mainclub: VfB Stuttgart 1893 e. V.

Capacity: 54.000

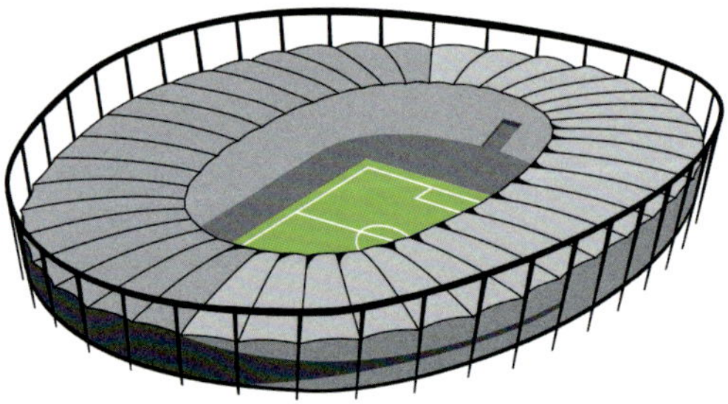

KÄRCHER
KÄRCHER

Das frühere Neckar-Stadion wurde 1933 nach den Plänen des Architekten Paul Bonatz erbaut. 1949-51 wurde eine offene Gegentribüne gebaut und 1955-56 folgte die Erweiterung der Cannstatter und Untertürkheimer Kurven. Weitere Ausbauten folgten 1971-73, 1974 (Haupttribüne), 1990 (Rasen). Das Gottlieb-Daimler-Stadion diente mit seinem Ringseildach, einer mit Polyestergewebe bespannten Konstruktion, als Vorbild für die Stadien in Frankfurt, Hamburg und Hannover.

The former Neckar Stadium was built in 1933 according to the plans of architect Paul Bonatz. From 1949-51, a public, opposing grandstand was built, and in 1955-56, the Cannstatter and Untertürkheimer curves were expanded. Further expansion work was performed in 1971-73, 1974 (main grandstand) and 1990 (turf). The Gottlieb Daimler Stadium, with its membrane roof stretched over a steel cable structure, served as a model for the stadiums in Frankfurt, Hamburg and Hanover.

L'ancien « Neckar-Stadion » a été construit en 1933 d'après les plans de l'architecte Paul Bonatz. Entre 1949 et 1951, une tribune est construite, à ciel ouvert, face à la tribune principale, suivie en 1955-1956 de l'agrandissement des virages Cannstatt et Untertürkheim. D'autres transformations sont effectuées en 1971-73, 1974 (tribune principale) et 1990 (pelouse). Avec son toit en matière textile (polyester), soutenu par une structure formée d'un cerceau central d'où partent des rayons, le « Gottlieb-Daimler-Stadion » a servi de modèle pour la construction des stades de Francfort, Hambourg et Hanovre.

El antiguo Neckar-Stadion fue construido en 1933 según los planos del arquitecto Paul Bonatz. Entre 1949 y 1951 se construyó una “contratribuna” abierta, y entre 1955 y 1956 se ampliaron las curvas de Cannstatt y Untertürkheim. Siguieron otras ampliaciones entre 1971 y 1973, en 1974 (tribuna principal) y en 1990 (césped). Con su techo de fibra de poliéster recubierta de PVC con un sistema radiado de sujeción, el Estadio Gottlieb-Daimler ha servido de modelo a los estadios de Francfort, Hamburgo y Hanóver.

L'ex Neckar-Stadion fu costruito nel 1933 secondo i piani dell'architetto Paul Bonatz. Dal 1949 al 51 fu costruita una tribuna all'aperto dalla parte opposta; durante il 1955-56 seguì l'ampliamento delle curve di Cannstatt e di Untertürkheim. Ulteriori ampliamenti furono eseguiti dal 1971 al 73, nel 1974 (tribuna principale) e nel 1990 (campo da gioco). Il Gottlieb-Daimler-Stadion con il suo tetto fatto di un tessuto di poliestere sospeso a funi ed anelli, serviva da modello per gli stadi di Francoforte, Amburgo ed Anovra.

O antigo Neckar-Stadion foi construído em 1933, segundo planos do arquiteto Paul Bonatz. Entre 1949-51 foi construída uma arquibancada oposta, aberta e em 1955-56 foram ampliados os setores conhecidos como Cannstatter e Untertürkheimer. Outras ampliações foram efetuadas em 1971-73, 1974 (arquibancada principal) e 1990 (gramado). A construção do telhado, revestido com um tecido de poliéster, serviu de modelo para os estádios em Frankfurt, Hamburgo e Hanover.

BW
BW Bank
weru Fenster+Türen weru
hlx.com
GEK Mir geht's gut!
67 a
c d

weru Fenster + Türen weru
Ensinger
nsequent Porsche.
LBBW
e
d
b

18b
18a

OTE
VfB Stuttgart

INDEX

Ove Arup & Partners (SE) | Berlin
www.arup.com
Allianz Arena

asp Architekten Arat-Siegel & Partner | Stuttgart
www.asp-stuttgart.de
Gottlieb-Daimler Stadion

Engels und Partner (SE) | Dortmund
www.engels-ingenieure.de
Signal Iduna Park

Fiebiger GmbH Architekten + Ingenieure | Kaiserslautern
www.fiebiger.com
Fritz-Walter-Stadion

Glöckner Architekten | Nuermberg
www.gloeckner.de
Zentralstadion

gmp Architekten von Gerkan, Mark und Partner | Hamburg
www.gmp-architekten.de
Commerzbank Arena
Olympiastadion
RheinEnergieStadion

Herzog de Meuron | Basel
Allianz Arena

HPP Hentrich-Petschnigg & Partner Architekten | Düsseldorf
www.hpp.com
Frankenstadion
Veltins Arena

KHP König, Heunisch und Partner (SE) | Frankfurt
www.khp-ing.de
Fritz-Walter-Stadion

IPL Ingenieure für Tragwerk und Leichtbau (SE) | Radolfzell
www.form-tl.de
Allianz Arena
Zentralstadion

Krebs und Kiefer (SE) | Darmstadt
www.kuk.de
Commerzbank Arena
Olympiastadion

Ingenieurbüro Köhler + Seitz (SE) | Nuremberg
www.koehler-seitz.de
Frankenstadion

Körber, Barton, Fahle | Freiburg
www.kbf-freiburg.de
Zentralstadion

Peter A. Kugler und Partner (SE) | Munich
www.drkugler.de
Zentralstadion

MOS Architekten | Hamburg
www.mosarchitekten.de
AOL Arena

Pelle Ingenieurbüro für Bauwesen (SE) | Dortmund
www.pelle-ingenieure.de
Veltins Arena

RFR Ingénieurs (SE) | Stuttgart
www.rfr-stuttgart.de
AWD Arena

Sailer Stepan und Partner (SE) | Munich
www.ssp-muc.com
Allianz Arena

Schlaich Bergermann und Partner (SE) | Stuttgart
www.sbp.de
Olympiastadion
Commerzbank Arena
Gottlieb-Daimler-Stadion
RheinEnergieStadion

Schröder Schulte-Ladbeck Strothmann | Dortmund
Signal Iduna Park

Schulitz + Partner Architekten | Braunschweig
www.schulitz.de
AWD Arena

Weideplan (SE) | Stuttgart
www.proplan-ingenieure.de
Gottlieb-Daimler-Stadion

Wirth + Wirth Architects | Leipzig
www.wirth-wirth.ch
Zentralstadion

WZ Ingenieure (SE) | Kaiserslautern
Fritz-Walter-Stadion

Joachim Fischer, Author

Born in 1960, employed as a freelance author and Communications and Design Consultant since 1990. He initiated the "Designers Saturday" in Stuttgart and Berlin and founded the design magazine "sign". www.brand-affairs.de

Thomas Hausberg, Graphic Design and Production

Born in 1953, his professional roots are in the areas of furniture and room design. In 2003, he established a publishing office with an emphasis on the conception of new print products, their design and production, including layout, imaging and the generation of print data and print monitoring. www.go4media.de

Dirk Wilhelmy, Photographer

Born in 1967, today he is one of the up-and-coming photographers. His pictures are used by leading book and magazine publishers. Half of his current success has to do with exploring the world of digital photography, the other half with his specialization in design and architecture. www.wilhelmy-fotografie.de

Thanks

We would like to thank the following persons for their support in the realization of this book: Christoph Meyer / Olympiastadion Berlin, Werner F. Goetz / Allianz Arena Munich, Fritz Lünschermann / Signal Iduna Park Dortmund, Gerd Voss / Veltins Arena Gelsenkirchen, Caspar Lindhorst / AOL Arena Hamburg, Marcel Boye / Commerzbank Arena Frankfurt, Hubert Röser / Rhein-Energie-Stadion Cologne, Mario Hohmann / Frankenstadion Nuremberg, Justin Ross / AWD Arena Hanover, Iris Rackwitz / Zentralstadion Leipzig, Michael Novak / Fritz Walter Stadium Kaiserslautern and Bernd Schmidt / Gottlieb-Daimler Stadium Stuttgart.

Picture Credits

The author wishes to thank the photographers Dirk Wilhelmy / Wilhelmy Fotografie Stuttgart, Robert Grahn / Euroluftbild Berlin and the illustrator Raphael Pohland / Stilradar, as well as the architects for their permission to reproduce the photographs and drawings. We have made every effort to pursue and protect the rights for the individual images. If, nevertheless, we have made an unintentional omission, we apologize to the photographers and architects.

published and distributed worldwide by
daab gmbh
friesenstr. 50
d-50670 köln

p +49-221-94 10 740
f +49-221-94 10 741

mail@daab-online.com
www.daab-online.com

publisher ralf daab
rdaab@daab-online.com

creative director feyyaz
mail@feyyaz.com

editior joachim fischer
fischer@brand-affairs.de

editorial coordination corinna mandic
editorial direction joachim fischer
editorial project by brand affairs stuttgart

introduction joachim fischer
translation ade team stuttgart

prepress thomas hausberg
thomas.hausberg@g-4-m.de

printed in germany by contzen print gmbh

isbn 3-937718-94-X